Is Heaven for Real?

I've Seen It and Don't Believe It

By Cathy Wilson
Copyright © 2014

Copyright © 2014 by Cathy Wilson

ISBN-13:
978-1500827182

ISBN-10:
1500827185

All Rights Reserved. No part of this publication may be reproduced in any form or by any means, including scanning, photocopying, or otherwise without prior written permission of the copyright holder.

First Printing, 2014

Printed in the United States of America

Income Disclaimer

This book contains business strategies, marketing methods and other business advice that, regardless of my own results and experience, may not produce the same results (or any results) for you. I make absolutely no guarantee, expressed or implied, that by following the advice below you will make any money or improve current profits, as there are several factors and variables that come into play regarding any given business.

Primarily, results will depend on the nature of the product or business model, the conditions of the marketplace, the experience of the individual, and situations and elements that are beyond your control.

As with any business endeavor, you assume all risk related to investment and money based on your own discretion and at your own potential expense.

Liability Disclaimer

By reading this book, you assume all risks associated with using the advice given below, with a full understanding that you, solely, are responsible for anything that may occur as a result of putting this information into action in any way, and regardless of your interpretation of the advice.

You further agree that our company cannot be held responsible in any way for the success or failure of your business as a result of the information presented in this book. It is your responsibility to conduct your own due diligence regarding the safe and successful operation of your business if you intend to apply any of our information in any way to your business operations.

Terms of Use

You are given a non-transferable, "personal use" license to this book. You cannot distribute it or share it with other individuals.

Also, there are no resale rights or private label rights granted when purchasing this book. In other words, it's for your own personal use only.

Is Heaven for Real?

I've Seen It and Don't Believe It

By Cathy Wilson

Table of Contents

Introduction 9
Heaven Defined 13
How the Mind Works 19
Protective Mechanism of the Brain 23
The Closest Proof - Near Death Experiences 27
Perceptions Changed 41
On Your Death Bed 45
Personal Experience - Ultimate Proof 51
Final Thoughts 55

Introduction

Is heaven for real? If I told you I had a black and white answer to that question I can guarantee you'd crap your pants, that's if you believed me. Obviously this is a subjective question, and depending on how open minded you are, added in your personal life experiences, will determine if you are a believer, non-believer, or whether or not there's any room for movement in your belief.

I want to share with you something that may sound "impossible" to you about two "life experiences that can be described as experiences crossing that line between life and death, that insanely scary divide simply because it's "the unknown." On two occasions in my life I was technically dead for a few moments. Where my physical body stopped, but my mind certainly didn't. I'll add to this I am not personally a believer of Heaven and Hell, which comes with God and religion.

I used to as a child, but my life experiences validated the belief in spirit and positive energy. In short you get back what you give, the more good things you do and positive you are, the more that comes back to you. I'm not going to get into that in this book, but what I experienced after having my truck squashed by a two ton truck, and when the anesthesiologist "accidently" gave me the wrong drug during a routine C-section, where on both occasions my heart and organs stopped, is unbelievable to me and I'm the one that lived through it.

My experiences where I truly believe I had the choice in my brain to give into the pain and die, for relief, or to choose life and deal with the surreal pain, opened my eyes to just how powerful the mind and body are when extremes unite. When all emotion is on red-alert, adrenaline pumping, sight, sound, scent, and feelings are heightened past their maximum, when the body is physically seriously stressed and damaged, is something I truly believe has no answer. A few moments where perhaps the body takes on a mind of its own and overrides you, the owner and caretaker of the physical.

I will talk a little more specifically about exactly what I experienced a little later, namely because for those of you that have the belief Heaven is real, I guess my personal experiences are as close as you can get to validating your belief. Ironic that it comes from a non-believer. I guess that's validation itself.
Do you think outside the box? Is your vision black and white, or rainbow?

Maybe the better angle is to ask you if there's proof there "isn't" heaven? Perhaps I should start by talking about how the world came to be, because without our actual physical world how can their possibly be a Heaven? Is there a Hell by default if I can convince you there is a Heaven?
What sort of validation is acceptable for you?

Do you need scientific evidence backed by studies, doctors, and other medical specialists that have signed off on the statement or group of conclusive facts?
Does any particular "real-life" experience qualify as proof to you?
Will my non-belief life experiences sway you?
How about sheer speculation that makes sense, or perhaps you are good with alternative health and wellness theories by qualified holistic practitioners?

My point here is this question: "Is Heaven for Real," can be answered a number of different ways. Whether you believe it or not is up to you. Just between you and me, it's probably in your best interest to believe in Heaven. In the least, this will give you something to look forward to after your time here on earth is finished. Just think about that for a minute.

Why not set yourself up positively for the terrifying unknown?
Near death experiences . . .
Scientists for one, will be the first to argue that near-death experiences are next to impossible, believing they may "feel" real, but are just brain fantasies coming to life.

Others believe that God and the soul are in fact real, and that death is just a transition phase in life, rather than an absolute. To me, that's putting a positive spin on the topic at hand, and there's no harm in that.

If your thinking dictates there's a Hell with a Heaven, and you are judged after your time on earth and sentenced to eternity, then you might not fare so well. My thinking is I've done a zillion things in my life that could easily send me "down" rather than "up," if in fact there is a judgment day, if Heaven is real, and if this means there is a Hell too, so the odds are not in my favor for a Happily Ever After.

Wow, that's a heck of a lot of "ifs" don't you think?

My head is spinning already, but no worries. I will make some sense of it all. My goal is to open your mind to the positive, where there's no harm in looking for the light at the end of the tunnel.

Perhaps my research and studies on the subject, along with my personal experiences, will give you the ammunition to find peace in your beliefs, or in the least give you a reason to consider that Heaven is for real.

First, let's start with the definition of heaven.

Heaven Defined

When talking about Heaven and what it is, you can't help but connect it with God and the Bible. This belief of Heaven suggests it's a place where God "lives." This majestically tranquil Utopia is calm and spiritual. In Christian terminology, it's recognized as the faithful place where Jesus, the stories of the Bible, God, and the likes interrelate and exist in harmony. It's a place of eternal happiness where pain doesn't exist, all sins are forgiven, and all burdens undone.

If you are granted the pass to Heaven, you get a new body that lasts for eternity. Many picture angels here. As with our world, there could very well be a hierarchy where there are "better" or "higher" levels of Heaven dependent on who you are, your beliefs and accomplishments in life. Most importantly, your acts of kindness towards others.

Biblically Defined . . .
Heaven means:
* "the abode of God and the angels."
* "the final destination for anyone that puts their heart and soul into faith."
* "the Earth's atmosphere."
In Hebrew, "Heaven" is *saymayuim*, meaning "heaved up things." If you look into the Greek New Testament, it's called *ouranos*, meaning "air or sky." In the Holy Scripture Heaven is called a number of different things including:
* "life everlasting"
* "the joy of the Lord"
* "great reward"
* "paradise"

I think you get the picture here.
If you are looking at Christianity you will see it defined as . . .
"The place where God resides which is prepared by Jesus and it's seen as "eternal bliss" far beyond our current knowledge. Entering Heaven grants you a new body that is everlasting. There isn't marriage in Heaven and varying levels of bliss are quite possible."

Again, all of these definitions are what you make of them, subjective and construed through your personal beliefs and experiences, ever-changing, if you will.

Looking into the Essence of Heaven, you will see more what heaven is "like," rather than what it is. It's central core where we will be in the presence of Jesus himself. Both Jesus and the Lord are in the Essence of Heaven, a paradise where we all who reside live in tranquil harmony. Think of "Heaven" as a single room in the mansion of "Essence."

Having faith gives you the ability to perceive Heaven to be everything you believe and more. With faith, you will experience a preview of what Heaven is. The journal is our life here on earth and the goal is to enter the gates of heaven to start living your perfect existence forever.

Many believe that living in Heaven means you are one with Christ, in the most utopian place possible, where everything and nothing exists simultaneously without question. All things positive are the reality here, where negativity doesn't show face, it just "isn't."

Is Heaven Real?
In general terms, we have created Heaven into a physical place that's very holistic and real. It's described in the Bible as a real place, and is mentioned in the New Testament 238 times. Don't quote me on that please.
By default, there is believed to be three Heavens, because a third Heaven is talked about.

So How do you Enter Heaven if Christian in Faith?
Upon dying, you are judged and this is where your afterlife is figured out. Think of it like going to court, where the concept of going to Heaven or Hell exists. You can be sinful, and if you ask for forgiveness, you will be granted a pass through the gates of Heaven. Sinners that don't ask for forgiveness, risk being directed to spend eternity in Hell.

This phase of judgment is different from the "final judgment," where Christ returns to judge everyone living and dead.
Heaven is the place where only the purest are allowed. If you die in a state of sin, you just can't enter. If you die in the good books with God, then you are cleansed and allowed to live in this heavenly Utopia forever. There are different scenarios of being granted an automatic pass into Heaven. For instance, if you have taken the oath of Chastity, as a monk or Catholic priest does, or if you've been baptized and die suddenly, those are the shortest routes to heaven in the Christian belief system.

The Existence of Heaven

Essentially, there is a Heaven if you believe in God and all this encompasses. Heaven goes hand in hand with this belief, and is recognized and acknowledged in the bible. It is the "guide" in which these believers look to live their lives.

Heaven Defined by Atheists . . .
There are extremists in all defined groups, although by definition atheism is just the lack of god-belief, not having atheism. Essentially, they just don't think about or care about religion as a whole, simply because atheists don't believe in God, they have no thoughts on Heaven or Hell. They believe Heaven is just a state of mind, and doesn't truly exist. Not wrong or right, just is.

Heaven Defined by Materialists . . .
Materialists simply don't believe that a personal spirit is able to spend the rest of time in Heaven or Hell. If you look at Heaven as a pure and material reality, this would be random without resolution into any set supernatural order the power of God, which raises the possibility that Heaven may actually exist in the thought process of Materialists. It's just what we need, some more "gray matter" here.

Heaven Defined by Pantheists . . .
Pantheists don't believe in an anthropomorphic or personal god. They think "everything" is God, if that makes sense. Pantheists focus on the now, and believe Heaven is what were are living here on earth. They don't focus on the afterlife, but you can believe if you wish. It's all about releasing your energy back into the universe as a whole to rise higher. Pantheists believe in Heaven, but it's much different to what Christians believe.

My Thoughts . . .
As you can see, Heaven is what you believe it to be. Your perceptions, experiences, and what you've been taught, will determine whether you believe in Heaven at all, and if you do, what sort of definition you have for it. The majority seems to

believe in the physical sense, it's a pure place of Utopia, where eternal happiness exists in harmony with nature, and the presence of religion is some shape or form, a system of beliefs.

How the Mind Works

It's important we understand the mechanics of the mind before we go further here. It's important, because the question of whether Heaven is Real or not, is dependent on perspective, and the power of mind, how your thought process works.

Your brain is unique and takes part in numerous tasks including:
* controlling heart rate, blood pressure, temperature and breathing
* taking care of your physical movement
* processing information about the world around you through your senses
* allowing you to reason, think, experience emotions, and dream

Your central nervous system is comprised of your brain, peripheral nerves, and spinal cord. This system is in charge of all your conscious and unconscious thoughts. It gathers all the information or evidence, which decides if you believe Heaven is real or not, for example.

Your brain has different sections controlling or monitoring your:
* Motor control
* Hearing
* Vision
* Learning
* Memory
* Emotions
* Sensations

A Little About How the Brain Evolved
We slowly manifested through the process of natural selection over time. The changes happened that were necessary for survival, they evolved. Three main stages are thought to have evolved with your thinking:

- The reptilian brain, innermost core (oldest)
- New functions and controls were added making the mammalian brain
- The neo-cortex, grey matter area of the brain is the newest
All divided into two hemispheres.

These three sections of the brain determine behavior and thought processes. Your thinking, perceptions, how you interpret things real or fantasy, how to create and justify your beliefs of Heaven, and whether or not the "proof" factor is required.

Will that even affect your personal belief?
The truth is, only you can answer that one.

Here's a little more on the mechanics of the brain, so you can connect the dots on why you might think the way you do, helping to better understand why you believe what you do, and how strong you are in that.

Is your mind open or closed to change?

Reptilian
The reptilian brain is thought to stay fairly consistent over time, as it controls the regulatory systems like breathing and body temperature, both necessary for life.

Mammalian
With the mammalian brain, came huge changes as mammals arose from reptiles. This brain has organs. There's more "awareness" with this brain, and storage developed. It's storage for memories through experience. This heightened the perception and awareness abilities evolving with brain development. In time, feelings of anger, fear, and other attachments developed from the intrinsic "fight or flight" response mechanism we know so well.

Human
With the human brain, massive amounts of gray matter manifested, consisting of the two hemispheres: The left controlling movement and sensations in the right side of your body. Of course, the left side of your body is controlled by the right brain.

Emerging with this brain is:
* Attachment feelings
* Fear
* Anger
* Behavioral responses due to feelings

Most people are right-handed, and the left side of the brain controls and organizes speaking. Whereas, the right side of the brain takes care of processing written language, and the actual understanding of words for the most part. Fascinating, don't you think? How do they interconnect to make it all work? The human brain is most complex, and evolved to be much more than the physics of just existing. It's complex in nature and purely powerful, much of which remains untapped or experienced.

My Thoughts . . .
What you can take from this, is there's always going to be the evolution factor with thinking, thought processes, processing information, gathering and storing facts, and so much more. Each of these processes are always going to be "fine-tuned." What has this got to do whether or not Heaven is real?
Your thinking, perceptions, feelings, and personal experiences all affect your beliefs and process of reasoning. They are subjective and multi-factorial, ever changing if you like. Your brain and the minute unique differences you have, even in your structural make-up, are going to influence your thoughts on Heaven, whether it exists, and if you need proof or not for validation. It's just something to ponder.

Protective Mechanism of the Brain

Fact - If a woman truly remembered the most intense moments of excruciating pain during childbirth, no woman would ever have more than one child. So how is it, that most women do it again and again? And in my case, six times so far?

Scientists believe the brain comes with a built-in bodyguard of sorts. It's protection that helps keep the brain from breaking down, or degenerating, and enables the brain to make minor repairs that help it function longer. We're not going to get technical here, and go into the science end of things, but this is important in your thinking and thought processes. What if you were influenced or pre-programmed to believe, or more likely to believe in manifestations of the mind, because of your intrinsic brain makeup?

It makes sense that women have some sort of built in mechanism to forget specific moments of the physical pain during childbirth, which enables a woman to magically consider having another baby.

A simple example might be that your brain structure and thinking, may be "made" to sway you further into the right hemisphere of your brain. Not so logical, but more likely to let your mind wander, consider, and see the possibility that Heaven exists.

Perhaps because of this, you actually "need" to have this belief more to validate yourself, your existence, and your life. More so anyway, than a person that has a little more neuron action on the left side of the brain. Predisposed to be a logical thinker more, and hence the "proof" Heaven is real, may be necessary, or required, in order to allow a person to believe.

Some people, depending on life experiences, environmental factors, and internal and external influences, may not even have the physical or mental ability to ever open their mind up to the possibility there's a Heaven. Never mind whether or not they need proof Heaven exists. Just think about it for a minute, never forgetting that your mind determines your reality.

My Thoughts . . .
What's important to understand, is that you may "think" you control your thinking the same as everyone else, but that's not quite true. You have no idea what base you start from. Your brain may be model 669, which has a few more brain cells in the right hemisphere than the previous model. Add to that your childhood experiences, which caused negative interference with the smooth processes of your logical brain. Which means it's now working at 90% efficiency.

Perhaps you add to that a strong religious upbringing, which tweaks your thoughts about Heaven more. Your reality is different from everyone else's. Not just because of external factors, but also intrinsic ones, factors that just may decide specific beliefs for you before you even start living life. I'm not trying to confuse you, but pry your mind open, and leave it that way.

The Closest Proof - Near Death Experiences

Did I tell you I "had" proof Heaven is real? Unfortunately, the people I knew that died were supposed to come back and let me know about all this Heaven stuff, but they stood me up! Cheesy I know.

My point is, you might as well accept the fact there is no black and white proof out there Heaven is real. So scientists might as well start walking now on this one.

1+1 does not equal 2 here.
The only proof of Heaven is through speculation, which is all individualized. Are you a dreamer? Do you go to church and believe in Christ? Are you afraid of death, and do you find warmth in allowing yourself to believe there is Heaven? Does the belief that Heaven is real help take the fear of dying away?

The closest there is to actually proving there is a Heaven in through a near death experience. It seems that when the mind gets into the hyper-sensitive "fight or flight" scenario of extreme stress, it protects and shifts to a tranquil or calm moment at just the right time. This explains why some people claim to have died and came back during a car accident, or even went to heaven when they flat-lined on the operating table, but were brought back to our physical world. It's a transition from the spiritual to the physical. What are your thoughts on this? Do you think these people are full of crap? That the stress of their deathly experience caused hallucinations to protect them and make them "think" they saw that calming bright white light? It's a theory scientists and other factoids seem to use more often than not.

This is where my life experiences fit in. There are many instances where you may not have the control you like, times unexpected where your physical, mental, and often intrinsic beliefs are challenged whether you like it or not. I will be brief with my descriptions because the purpose here is to describe those few moments when I believe my life crossed that uncertain line between life and death. The one people often wonder about, but most don't experience and live or choose to talk about it. I have 2 such experiences I'm ready to share.
I'll use KISS here, Keep It Simple Stupid, and mark them One and Two.

One
I was 20 weeks pregnant with my 6th child, a single mom, heading out for coffee with a friend. It was a wintery night, we had some freezing rain early in the day and the snow was falling quite steadily. My oldest was 13 at the time and very responsible. It was shortly after 7 pm, and I had all the kids snuggly in bed except for the oldest two. I was only expecting to be gone for about an hour. So I made them some popcorn, checked that my cell phone was on in case they needed to call me, and I bundled up and headed out the door. My Durango was in

rough shape, but it was big enough for all my kids and got me from A to B.

On a side note, the kids didn't know I was expecting at the time. I wanted to make sure everything was okay with the baby before I leaked the news. Actually, nobody knew except a couple of close friends at the time.

I headed out the lane and normally would have taken a left toward the highway that led into town. Instead I decided to take another road because my normal route looked a little crowded, and I knew it took forever to make the turn onto the highway anyway.

It was snowing harder than I thought, but I could still see for the most part, and knew the main roads were always pretty clear. It was only 5 minutes to the coffee spot in town anyway. I made the left onto the unfamiliar side street that took me down the hill to the highway. I made the left hand turn down the hill, about 40 feet to the stop sign at the bottom, where theoretically I would have make the right hand turn onto the highway.

Well it didn't quite go as planned. I remember making the turn at the top of the hill and riding my brakes down the hill because it was slippery, and I just wanted to creep down the hill, not to mention the snow was blowing pretty good too.

It all happened so fast it really was unbelievable at the time. I recall pushing harder on the brakes as I got closer to the bottom of the hill, and panic struck because my actions and the result wasn't adding up. I pressed harder, but my truck was picking up speed, which didn't make sense. I was sliding down the hill on ice with no traction to brake. Of course I didn't know that at the time.

The signal something was wrong, was my heart jumping out of my chest. You know the feeling, just like when you're driving along and hear the police siren come out of nowhere and scare the crap out of you.

It was a blur. I remember feeling lost, looking to my left and seeing a large white flash, then feeling a solid jolt that felt like the thought of punching a cat. Not that I want you to punch a cat, but that gives you an idea of the power of the impact. Disoriented, I was spinning and bouncing, didn't know what was going on. And it definitely didn't register that I'd just been smacked drivers side by a 2 ton truck driving through on the highway.

I must have blacked out, and when I came to, all I could feel was cold and panic. I had an all-encompassing sense of tiredness, and just wanted to close my eyes and rest for a minute, so I could get out and go check on my kids. The first thing that popped into my head for some reason was to go make sure the kids were alright, instinctive I guess. Perhaps my unconscious mind wanted to reassure them I was ok when I really wasn't.

My truck was totalled, a wrecked piece of metal that authorities say nobody should have come out alive from. A man that stopped to help smashed in the back window to get in, because the doors were crumpled shut. I remember him talking to me when all I wanted to do was close my eyes and rest. I was shivering uncontrollably and he put his black leather jacket on me as best he could.

I asked him to go check on my kids for me over and over. Probably trying to distract myself from bringing to a conscious level that I had just been in a serious car accident. He found my phone and reassured me the kids would be fine. He called my friend and told him what had happened, and told me help was on the way.

I guess I passed out for a bit and when I came to, the man was gone that I was talking to, and a paramedic was trying to hook some sort of harness on me to get me out. Of course asking me all sorts of questions I was too tired to answer. The pain in my body was unbearable and I just wanted it to stop.

The jaws of life were on the way to get me out, and I just kept asking for someone to go check on my kids. There were two fire trucks, three police cars, and a couple ambulances. I was so relieved when I heard someone confirm nobody else was in the car. 99.9 % of the time I've got most of my kids with me. I couldn't remember if I had them or not.

It was freezing cold, I was shivering and shaking, past the point of being able to deal with the pain. I didn't have a scratch on me, but my insides were literally killing me. I remember as the ambulance attendant was trying to lay me back to get me out, begging him to sit me upright because I couldn't breathe when he did that. He wasn't listening and I was starting to consciously panic. The scariest thing I ever experienced was not being able to breathe full breathes in deeply.

They had no choice and had to get me out now. With all the confusion, lights flashing in my eyes, the death cold, I felt head to toe, and the unbearable pain I was feeling, so much so that it encompassed me, pushed me to the point of making the ultimate decision, I had to make the choice, the one that surfaces only under extremely heightened conditions mentally and physically, with a specific circumstance.

The choice to live or die…
At this moment in time, it didn't matter that I was an overly positive person, that I had a loving and supporting family, and that people depended on me, and I lived to please others. None of it mattered.

The emergency team finally got me into the ambulance, and as the seconds past, it felt like they were piling more elephants on my chest. It was getting harder and harder to breathe, I was *tired of all the surface questions from the ambulance attendants, the lights shining in my eyes, and most of all the pain. I was at the point where I would do anything to just stop the pain. It seemed like all this was lasting for hours, but it was only minutes in real time. To me it felt like everything was moving in slow motion, with the one constant of pain increasing with intensity.*

I decided I wasn't going to listen to the attendants to keep my eyes open and "stay with them." I was tired and sick of fighting for my next breathe. All I wanted was for the pain to stop so I could sleep.

I consciously closed my eyes, which I later learned was when I flat-lined. When I closed my eyes I saw a flash of bright white light. I didn't see any angels and it wasn't like I was at the gates of Heaven or anything else like that. But there was light and I felt a warmth circulate through me, warming me up, which was a welcome relief from the intense cold I was feeling, so cold it actually hurt.

I remember being drawn to this warm energy, not questioning what it was or why it was happening. I had a feeling inside so wonderful I didn't want it to end, and I really didn't care about anything else except what I was feeling. There was no room for any other thought, at least that's the way it seemed.

Nothing was said and I didn't see anyone, but I knew there was a choice to be made. Don't ask me how, I just knew. Every fiber of my being wanted to stay warm and be rid of the pain, nothing else mattered. I was allowed to rest with this thought for what seemed like a few hours, but in reality couldn't have been more than a few seconds.

Then suddenly the deep loving feelings I had for my kids popped into my head. Which hurt worse than the pain of not being able to breathe. I thought about how hurt they would be without me around, and that very thought was killing me. My job was to protect and love them no matter what.

I didn't recognize it at the time, but in those few seconds I was making the choice to live or die. Death was very inviting and I truly believe if it wasn't for the thoughts of my children I would have graciously chosen death. But I couldn't hurt my children and consciously chose to deal with the pain and live. The second I told my mind this, I gained consciousness again and felt the unbearable pain cut through me, the physical pain of my collapsed lung. I made the decision to live because the pain I would have felt leaving my children, was worse than any sort of physical pain I had to endure.

I made the choice to live, but will never forget the fact I was seconds away from making the decision to willingly die.

Two
This next incident happened just 5 months later when I was actually delivering my 6th child. I was still on the mend from my car accident, but in pretty good shape considering. I credit that to making sure I ate well and trained daily at the gym.

So I took my two oldest children with me to the delivery. Initially they were both going to come into the operating room when their little brother was being delivered by c-section. But for some unconscious reason, I decided it was better if they just waiting in the waiting area. The father wasn't in the picture and I figured I was okay, just going in alone. The nurses and doctors were great and supportive, and I was focusing on how excited my kids would be to hold their new baby brother minutes after he was born. That thought was simply amazing to me.

I needed to show my children I was strong. That's just me. So I was prepped for the delivery, very relaxed and excited. The anesthesiologist came in and talked about the basics of the procedure with me. I have really low blood pressure, which was a concern for them because the epidural they were giving me would slow down my heart. That's good for most people, but not me. So they pumped me full of fluids and had syringes of adrenaline to give me in a timed fashion throughout the delivery. The idea was this would counteract the effects of the epidural and give my heart the boost it needed to stay pitter-pattering.

I trusted they had it all figured out, and was relaxed and ready to get on with it.
I got numbed from the waist down and even teased the doctor when he poked my legs and asked if I could feel it. I said OUCH when they should have been numb. He figured it out, laughed and gave me crap at the same time.

He started and all was well.
I had a woman from the resuscitation room right beside me doing some surface talk to keep my mind busy and out of the worry-zone. I remember feeling a little queasy, which was normal, but this queasiness persisted and inside my head I as getting worried. I sensed something was wrong by didn't know what, only that my head was screaming panic and I remember thinking they just had to get the baby out. Not sure why at the time, but that's what I was thinking.

Before the doctor made his first cut the buzzers started going off. Panic rose and I heard the doctors saying they didn't know what was going on, but they were losing me. So the surgeon was asking if he should proceed with the delivery fast, and the anesthesiologist and other doctors were yelling no, they needed to figure out what was going on.

I remember laying there and I couldn't breathe no matter how hard I tried. I couldn't blink or move a muscle even though in my head I was screaming for help. I could hear and see all the chaos around me, but couldn't even blink to let them know I was conscious.

Dead alive is exactly what I was.
I couldn't answer any of their panicked questions or respond to the bright lights flashed in my eyes. I was trapped and thought for certain I was going to die. I couldn't understand why the doctors couldn't hear me and why they weren't giving me air. I was begging and pleading in my mind, but they weren't listening or responding. At that point, I switched my thinking to my unborn baby. I started screaming in my head they needed to get my baby out now, that he needed to be okay and I really didn't care about what happened to me. He needed to be safe and alive and if I had to die for that to happen, at that point in time I was ready.

Again, it was the pain that was dictating my thoughts and actions. I flat-lined for a few seconds and I found out afterwards this was because the anesthesiologist gave me the wrong drug. It was a paralyzer they were giving me instead of the adrenaline I needed. It temporarily stopped all my organs until the drug wore off. Luckily it wasn't a larger dose or I would have literally suffocated on the table while consciously aware.
The doctors didn't know at the time of the drug mistake. They thought I was having some sort of heart failure.
During the few seconds I flat-lined, I remember that bright light again, a beautiful brilliant inviting warm light under the circumstance. It had some sort of magnetic power that draws you in without question, like it somehow hypnotizes you and willingly you'd do whatever it asked, not thinking about anything else except how you were feeling.
For the second time in my life, I believe I had a choice. To continue suffering with the terror of not breathing, a pain most unbearable, or to deal with, no air so that my son could be born. Once again the thought of not actually getting to meet my little one was worse than not having the ability to breathe. I knew I could deal with the physical pain, but I couldn't deal

with the thought of not getting to meet my son, and having him grow up not knowing how much I loved him.

I chose the pain again and when I did, I was given hope. At that point, I still figured I was going to die, until I felt a squeak of air slip into my suffocating lungs, not enough to get even a half breath, but enough to give me hope. The drug was wearing off and with the oxygen mask on my face, little by little the air was being pushed into my lungs. Words can't describe the happiness I felt, like Christmas a million times over.

Within a few minutes I came to, and it felt and was acting like I just had a stroke. My speech was jumbled and slowed, and I couldn't really move my head or arms yet, but it was coming back.

When I was able to, I communicated to the doctors to get my son out now while I was still numb from the waist down, because they weren't getting me up on the table again. They wanted to wait because they thought it was my heart and didn't determine till the next day if was a drug mistake.

My son was born and I was in really rough shape, but managed to hide it from my children and focus on what meant everything to me, and that was watching them oogle over their new baby brother.

These are two separate instances where even though I'm not personally a believer in Heaven, I do believe I had the choice to live or die, and the circumstances line up with individuals claiming to have life/death experiences that are also interconnected with the Gates of Heaven.
…
Perhaps you believe there is substance in these individuals that have crossed the gap between reality and imagination, those that have through no choice of their own crossed into the spirit

of energy and back to the physical of reality. Better yet, how to you prove this one way or another?

I believe the only "proof is in the word of those who have experienced it.

It's not like you can videotape the mind. Even then, how can that be proof because the mind does have imagination. How do you sort reality from not? Yikes - talk about stirring the pot here.

Let's first look into people that have been clinically dead and believe they have experienced Heaven and have proof of it. My experiences fit right in here, except the part about actually experiencing Heaven, in my mind anyway.

What happens is people perceive or interpret this experience to their beliefs, differing religions and cultures, for example, will describe "Heaven," or this visit to the other side differently. The majority of people clinically dead describe this experience as seeing a "being of light."

A Christian may have seen Jesus, and a Buddhist may meet another figure of importance. Even here, there are differences based on life experiences, thinking, and how the brain gathers and processes information.

From these experiences, the conclusions are mostly descriptions of proof of Heaven, depict Heaven as more of a non-physical place. It's not like you would describe a coffee shop: With walls, a roof, floor, tables and chairs. If you were to put a physical into this description, it would be bright white light. The physical isn't like a chair, but rather a cloud of bright light. It's already telling you this is a sensory description with heightened awareness and senses. It's communicated through thoughts and perceptions using subjective imagination. There is no ability to describe Heaven in the black and white, such as it is a huge white house with white marble floors and cloud beds in every room. Structure as we know and relate to, just isn't the reality of Heaven. At least, in the experience of most that have had life-death experiences, it's not concrete one might say, which increases skepticism.

"Bright iridescence" is one description used. A "feeling' they were in Heaven, or that God was there, and that was enough for them to believe and have proof of Heaven. Having this experience opens the mind to the fact that Heaven is much more than a physical presence. In fact, most of us base understanding, validity, and belief, on the physical.

The thoughts of people that have proof of Heaven, are that the physical doesn't matter, because it's the spiritual, and the metaphysical that means everything. This is very different thinking than what most of us are used to. This experience is essentially beyond anything most can process, because they haven't experienced being "clinically dead," and had the experience to push their sensory perceptions into another realm altogether, where physical doesn't matter because the power of perception and sensory recognition is everything, where the power of the mind is all the focus, and proof really isn't needed for such an experience.

Maybe we need proof for everything because we are so limited in thought, in experiencing the true power of the mind and what matters?

Maybe these people didn't really experience Heaven, but rather the bright light most speak of is just like the warm-up to Heaven. Maybe that's the lobby of the building, that has the elevator to Heaven? Close, but not quite there. Speculation I know, but at least this speculation has some true believers in unique life-death experiences to validate.

Some believe this "bright light" is actually behind God, before you die and enter Heaven, heightened imagination and sensory overload. It's a positive stress on the system during extreme circumstances, which makes the mind go into default and produce a vision of white light for protection? The sky is the limit in explanation, but regardless there are those that believe their experience is proof of Heaven. To them it is. The jury is still out on the verdict for everyone else.

Here are some more commonalities between people that experienced a life-death scenario.

* Light experience
* Something deeper in the heart of the whole experience
* Experienced calm, peace, joy, tranquility
*Urgency and extreme circumstance

The proof of Heaven here, is that many people have had similar, yet different experiences, and the fact remains they are associated closely enough to be valid. They are proof of Heaven, an emotional experience that gives a strong solid impression of extreme heightened awareness.

In other words, the experience here is enough to believingly describe the "essence" of Heaven, what it's like, which can only happen if it truly exists. These experiences focus or exhibit characteristics that are very personalized in nature. One person describes the feeling of the white light as an incredibly joyful and happy feeling of the recognition of going home, one so strong he would have followed the light expected to go home, but not really caring at all about the destination, but rather loving the journey.

My grandmother once told me life isn't about the destination, but rather being grateful for every joyous minute of the journey. It's your recollection of journeys when all is said and done, that holds value.

Some experts relate the "white light" with a state of consciousness. Meeting past relatives for example, in this light is an extended state of consciousness, with formless and pure light. This light seems to be non-physical, where the light experienced isn't from "other worlds," but rather these other worlds have their own unique origin from this single bright light.

This belief of Heaven, is both subjective and interconnected with personality, different for everyone. Best understood when an open mind that universally accepts all parameters of life and belief, is the ultimate. So, if you are narrow minded in thinking, even if you do believe in Heaven and Jesus, you are less likely to understand Heaven and accept proof of it, simply because Heaven isn't one belief, thought, or physical place. It is a melody of emotion, thoughts, feelings, experiences, perceptions, and spirituality. Heaven is an "essence" from which you can create. So all you need is proof of this essence to make Heaven a reality, and that we have. Think about it.

My Thoughts . . .
You can't explain illogic with logic. It's tough to open a mind sealed shut with narrow mindedness. If you need proof of Heaven, is your thinking open enough to actually believe there is or could be a Heaven? Maybe Heaven is not a place, but rather a thing. It's something visited and experienced, but not located. An "essence" of pure joy, love, calm, and heightened spiritually bliss on all levels, stimulating every sensory outlet beyond what any one of us could ever imagine. Again, your reality is what you think, create, and ultimately believe.

Perceptions Changed

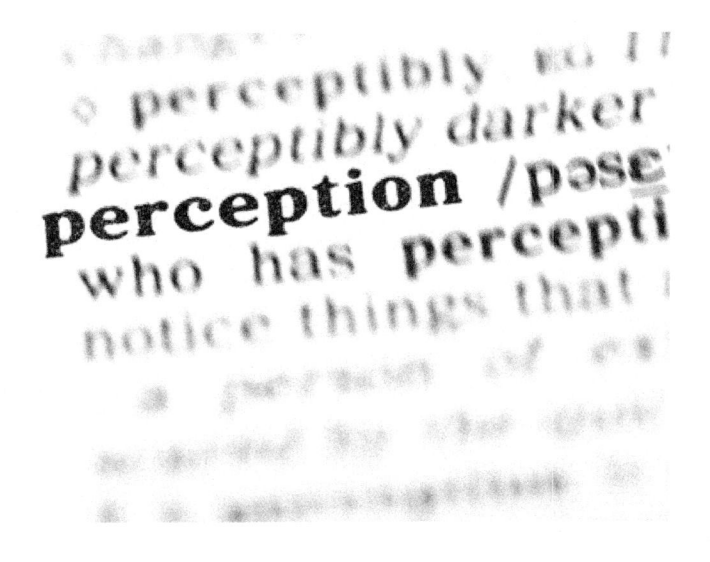

Experiences influence perception. Your perceptions are always changing, and you dictate through your thoughts, actions, and beliefs, how you see and receive information. Perception is the process where your senses translate stimuli into meaning. Philosophers are the "go-to" guys on this term. They love to answer questions with questions, and they often question of source of human knowledge, how, and if it's valid or not. An open-ended subjected thought in itself don't you think?

If you look at perception on a more scientific angle, the definition is more exotic. It's the process of gathering, interpreting, choosing, and categorizing information attained through your senses. Cognitive scientists, yikes, believe as we experience the world, we are objective about the world itself, but our perceptions are created through our senses, with provision.

Looking from a contemporary psychological view, perception is your brain's interpretation of all information brought to light through your senses, for the purpose of finding meaning.

Bottom line is, your senses; sight, sound, touch, talk, and listen, are used to make conclusions. You take in information as gathered through your senses, and decide on the meaning. A simple example is, you may perceive a fire to be hot. Why? Well, you can feel the heat from the fire, and in your experience "heat" means hot. You also remember touching fire as a child, and feeling physical pain because of this. Your brain remembers all of your experiences for protection and learning. Even though many aren't at a conscious level until needed, your brain can only store so many thoughts in your conscious, and "take-action" memory. The thoughts and experiences not relevant to the situation, are put away in your filing cabinet of unconscious thoughts, collecting dust until your brain needs them again for something.

There are all sorts of different theories and forms of perception, depending on what angle you are looking from. We are going to have a look at perception and reality, because it's important in looking for the evidence Heaven is real.

Perception and Reality
Here the belief is, as we experience "life," our perception and understanding of things shifts. This makes sense. You may love dogs, having only experienced happiness with them. One day a dog may bite you and caused you harm. Now your perception that all dogs are harmless and loving has changed. It took an experience different from what you are used to, in order to change your perception. This thinking backs up the belief Heaven may be something you believe in or don't, because of your personal life experiences and processing of them through your senses. This may also determine if you need proof of Heaven to validate its existence. If you aren't planning on dying anytime soon, maybe you aren't going to have any

perceptive thoughts on the topic. It's a conscious choice that will change in time.

My Thoughts . . .
How you perceive all things in life reflects what you believe and what you think to be hogwash. Some people develop absolute perceptions of specific topics, backed by validations only making sense to themselves. For instance, you may know of someone that says they hate all gay people, just because they developed these perceptions or this belief growing up as a child. They don't care about taking the time to get to know these people before forming their belief. The perception is what it is, because they won't allow change. This closed mind to thought, probably has a solid belief already on whether there is a Heaven or not, and/or whether or not they need proof of Heaven. So, for this person, it really doesn't matter what I write or don't write, their mind is pre-maturely decided.

On Your Death Bed

This is where one has to step up to the plate. You may have lived your life with a "tough-man" personality, where nothing could ever take you down, like you could do it all yourself, and really didn't need anyone to lean on. I know, I've been there and sometimes still doing that. Regardless, I am nobody to judge, but more often than not when people reach the finish line, the moment where they truly know they are going to die, panic sinks in.

Is this really the end? Is there a Heaven? What do I need to do in order to get to Heaven? Do I come back at some point as another form? Am I going to Hell? When I die is that really the end of the road?
Perhaps death is just the beginning? Think about that for a minute.

Death can be defined as the cessation of all biological functions which help sustain a specific living organism. It's pretty straight forward.

Causes of death include:
* Predation
* Malnutrition
* The Natural Aging Process
* Murder
* Suicide
* Disease
* Accidents
* Trauma causing terminal injury

There are people that "say" they believe when they die that's the end, even when they are moments away from it. Deep down, my belief is there is a hope within them they are wrong, and that even after death there will be more living, regardless of the pain and turmoil they may have faced in their human existence.

A belief, it would be a nice surprise if there was a Heaven, and that they were on their way to visit, even though they firmly believe this not to be the case. As humans we are allowed to change our minds, and sometimes when we lose control, perhaps when death is near, this often triggers a change in thinking, one that opens up the mind and contemplates there is more to life, that it can't possibly just end when it's seemingly just begun.

Just think the evolutionary "fight or flight' response. You are reacting unconsciously to what your body is relaying to you intrinsically, without control. The same basic scenario repeats itself when you are going to die. Fear, unknowing, absolute, anxiety and wonder, hit you simultaneously, and this is likely to push you into believe anything at that particular moment.

This explains why many people will turn to Christ suddenly. They will ask for forgiveness, and offer to do anything in exchange for mercy. Their mind has evolved and changed over time, and because there emotion is everything just before death, or as it approaches, they try to quickly figure out a way to control this overwhelming fear, to convince themselves the end is not really here, and perhaps open their mind to going to Heaven, where death is only the beginning of life. A valid life scenario to consider.

The Deeper Meaning Behind Death . . .
We only gain by considering there is deeper meaning behind death, that it's not an absolute, a dark ending, but rather a bright light, a pathway leading to a new and joyously pure beginning, a beginning that never ends.

As humans, we are spiritual beings that have experience being human, not human beings with spiritual experience. Although similar, these are two very different trains of thought. We are going to work with the belief we are spiritual beings, simply because there is so much more to life than what we have experienced as humans. We are multi-dimensional and extend light years beyond our five sense and "life" experiences.

Transition into the Light . . .
Life isn't just about what you see, hear, feel, touch, and taste. Open your mind to the possibility death, transitions you into the light, in which you can return into your original state of purity. The white light you are thinking of right now, is a signal of your being in its natural form - pure, innocent, loving, compassionate, calm, and giving. You return to your spirit from which you started, maybe only to begin again, or spend an eternity in your all wonderful spiritual form.

Your human body may just be a vehicle for gaining knowledge good and bad. It's a way for you to evolve and grow as a human, gathering information to take back with you when you return to you, your soul purest, your original for that exists for evermore. Think it's worth considering?

Society has shaped us to fear death, to equate it to dark, evil, Hell, turmoil, and pain. Humans aren't good with the unknown, and of course death is exactly that. The unknown factor makes us pay attention to the fact we are vulnerable in life. That, in itself, is scary. We may be able to avoid death and prolong life for a time, but death is inevitable. Something every human being has in common with one another.

As humans if we don't "know" something, we will often discount, avoid, or criticize. This somehow makes us feel more in control or valued, "better." As a society, we shun death because we close our mind to the positive light of it. We see it as an ending absolute, dark, scary, negative, and sad.

Maybe if you open your thinking to understand there is a deeper meaning in death, you might see the light. This might help to create clarity and understanding, perhaps finding wisdom. Opening our minds to the thought of Heaven may be a sign as humans we "want" to understand death, and find the deeper meaning. It just seems we skip over the topic of death completely, and look to the light of Heaven.

Many people don't need proof of Heaven, because on their death bed the alternative is dark and fearing. **Behind door number one** you can have death as humans see it. The ending, absolute, after which there is nothing more.

Door number two is the thought of Heaven. The possibility there is more to life after death: A place so spiritually pure, calm, and loving, where people would flock to if only they knew. Perhaps this is why "death" is something that happens to everyone, simply because every person on the face of the earth deserves to visit what we call Heaven. This way, not one person is denied, except maybe of course if they have chosen to live their life with evil. Then perhaps they lose the privilege of heaven, and go straight to Hell. Quite possible don't you think?

What truly matters in life . . .
If we didn't "lose" things in life, we wouldn't recognize gain or appreciate the enriched wisdom we receive through tragic times, in death, or turmoil. The important life lessons are learned through death, where we are reminded that the way we live our lives, basing our value and status on material possessions, knowing and "having more," that in death, all we have accumulated and accomplished is meaningless.

In an instant, a whole life of experiences can mean absolutely nothing. This is only experience in death. Do you think a person cares how much money they have in the bank on the day they die? Or how many people are friends on their Facebook? Having six vacation houses and six exotic cars parking in the drive, means absolutely nothing when you are facing death.

What matters is the love, compassion, and warm memories around you. Death teaches us how to be compassionate and loving. The "emotion" of your human life is what matters. That is something that will stay with you, and become your "gold." How you treated others and the compassionate offerings of yourself, how great they make you feel inside are what matters. That's where the value is measured in your time on earth. It seems very unfair, and most don't recognize this until it's too late to turn back the clock. They don't recognize this, how simple life could have been and how utterly fulfilling it would have been, if only. It's not until a person is about to breath their last breath that "life" makes sense.

A signal death is really the beginning of life? Maybe.

My Thoughts . . .
As humans we all understand we will die one day. This is a reality we are taught to fear, and try and wish away. You only

know what you know, perhaps opening our mind to the possibility that your death bed is not just that, the end, is constructive. By changing your perception and believe surrounding death to a positive light, you may fare better in life itself. Death doesn't have to be dark. We just choose it to be.

Personal Experience - Ultimate Proof

I'm the first to admit I have never had much faith or belief, in any sort of spiritual or out-of-body experience people claim. I went to church as a little girl, but don't really have thoughts one way or another about God, the church, Heaven or Hell. Actually, I sometimes joke with my friends, and voice it doesn't really matter if there is a Heaven, because I'm going the other direction anyway. I've sinned, and don't sinners go to Hell? I can't imagine ever getting "forgiveness" anyway, for all the mistakes I have made.

However, my surreal experiences that have opened my mind and heart to the thoughts of Heaven, something after we are finished our time on earth.

The Choice
I truly believe the only thing that stopped me from death experiences was my children. I was the caretaker and provider for all my children. They needed me and I needed them. I was there for everything, and they for me. Just the thought of dying and leaving them to fend for themselves, not being there to cook and clean for them, to take care of them, was like a knife in my heart.

The simple thought of that, brought a sorrow so deep, immediate tears to my face and an emotional pain much stronger than the physical pain I was experiencing, that I was happily willing to take death for.

It was a conflict of feelings and thoughts without interference, the black and white of my life, at a moment in time when my life was as a physical and mental crossroad.

My Pain vs. My Children
I couldn't handle the pain of the "thought" of dying on my children. I remember that pain and wanted it gone. At that point, I knew I could deal with the physical pain as long as the thought of leaving my children didn't become a reality. I questioned whether or not a bond or life purpose, a love could be so strong. My situation answered this question.

I made the choice to live. Slowly, I let the voices of the anxious and stressed out paramedics come back into my head, and reluctantly I allowed that unbearable pain in too. The pain I was truly ready to die for. As I did this, I remembered the bright white light fading and I didn't feel the pain of "thinking" I would make my children sad by dying, because I only had room in my head for the real pain I was feeling in my chest. I'd be lying if I told you I understood all of this, particularly at the time, because I most definitely didn't. I was just reacting to what was in front of me.

Looking back now, I believe that very well could have been the doorstep to heaven. If it was, then I can tell you right now you have ZERO reason to be afraid of death. When you are ready and you choose to die or leave this earth, you are only going to experience amazing, a warmth, and magnetic existence of positive that focuses on an energy and spirit of goodness.

Something so magnificent and beyond the understanding of our limited brains, that one might think if they knew this for sure before it was your time to die, you might have chosen sooner. That's just not the way it works though.

If we were able to experience Heaven before actually experiencing death, completely, and absolutely, we might rather be happy and celebrate when a loved one dies, simply because we know they are going to a fabulous "essence" for eternity. It's not a place, but rather a space. It's a space in time where all joy is found in pure existence. Not measured with successes, money, and materialistic things, like we do today.

I believe if Heaven is real, it's an absolute of Utopia, a state of mind that is perfect forever. Heaven is whatever you believe it to be and so much more, all in a positive and pure light.
Like it or lump it, but I know I'm never getting any more proof of Heaven than that.

My Thoughts . . .
Five years ago this question of Proof of Heaven would have confused me. Through my "challenging" life experiences, for whatever reason, I have learned Heaven could be real. My belief is pure and true, something that empowers me to make the most of every moment I have on earth in order to prepare myself, my heart and soul wholly for the beginning of life, which begins after death in a divine and pure place many humans call Heaven.

For me, I really don't need a label, and I don't care to spend my life focusing on "the next chapter,' if there is one. It is what it is and I'm content leaving it at that.

Final Thoughts

Is there proof of Heaven? Well scientific experiences of "clinical death" experiences don't prove Heaven exists. They are thoughts, feelings, perceptions, and opinions based on personal experiences that are intrinsic, of the mind, and can't be tested or challenged, the only route to scientific proof.

This is a subjective question, which means each one of us can create and validate a correct answer. Your reality is what you make it.

Consider the fact proof of Heaven exists around us. Look at animals, for example. Animals don't sin, and they don't possess evil. They kill only to eat, and it's humans that interfere and cause harm. A dog wouldn't normally bite without reason. However, it may bite if an abusive person has taught it that.

From a religious perspective, this thought alone validates proof of Heaven.

Humans are evil, but animals are not. If a wild tiger kills a man it the wilderness, it's because it is hungry and wants to eat, not because it wants to commit murder. Man kills to commit murder. If a sand shark takes a bite out of a surfer, it's not because he wants to cause pain or harm. It's because the sand shark was hungry, and looking to fill this instinctive biological need.

Your mind, how it works, your existence and experiences, religious beliefs and practices, the willingness of your mind to evolve with time, are all factors determine your beliefs.
For me personally, I don't need proof of Heaven. I saw and experienced, what some may believe to be Heaven, but I don't need validation one way or the other.

It makes sense that death has been misunderstood in the human world. Death doesn't have to be dark and sorrowful, bringing forth feelings of fear and insecurity, an absolute. By attempting to see death in a positive light, we open our mind to search for and accept a deeper meaning to death. Death may be the beginning of life, perhaps just a vehicle in which each one of us gathers information, and experiences to serve a higher purpose of understanding, far greater than any limited experiences we've have with our five senses.

As humans, we tend to be skeptical, disbelievers without scientific validity. Yet, we know the power of the mind is so much more. Your imagination is just an example. Look into the power of your thoughts and feelings. You can create, dream, and experience through imagination, anything you want. So, why can't we open our mind in death and life to "greater?"

You control you, your thoughts, feelings, perceptions, and beliefs. Or do you?

Maybe it's time we stopped spending our human lives fearing death, and look to opening our minds to exploring and understanding it, looking beyond the inevitable, and finding meaning and good. There's something pure and surreal beyond death, which is just the gateway to a heavenly world. Maybe then you will have your proof of Heaven, if that's what you need.
"Your eternal spirit is more real than anything physical in the human world, and it's your ever-loving spirit that connects wholly with what we humans define as "Heaven." The place many aim to return to, back to our spiritual self." . . . the beginning.
Do you believe?

Last Thoughts…

*__THANK-YOU__ for reading my masterpiece. I hope you learned a little something, or at least got a few smiles.
*I would appreciate a millisecond or three of your time for a quick review, to help me build my masterful book empire higher.
*Whatever you do, don't forget to smile, and of course, check out my website for more of my e-Book masterpieces!
www.flawlesscreativewriting.com

Cathy☺

Disclaimer

All Rights Reserved Copyright © 2014 Cathy Wilson

No part of this book can be reproduced, stored, or transmitted by any means including recording, scanning, photocopying, electronic or print without written permission from the author. While utmost care has been taken to ensure accuracy of the written content, the readers are advised to follow the guidelines and ideas mentioned herein at their own risk. The author in no case shall be responsible for any personal or commercial damage that results due to misinterpretation of information.

This book does not take personal situations into consideration, and therefore may not be fit for every purpose. All readers are encouraged to seek professional advice for a specific situation.

Printed in Great Britain
by Amazon

43504280R00036